No Lex 10-12

Juliet Heslewood

INTRODUCING

PICASSO

Little, Brown and Company
Boston   Toronto   London

First U.S. Edition
Developed and produced by Belitha Press Ltd.,
31 Newington Green, London, England N16 9PU,
1993

Library of Congress Cataloging-in-Publication Data
  Introducing Picasso / Juliet Heslewood. — 1st
U.S. ed.
    p.   cm.
Summary: Examines the life of the well-known modern painter and the historical and artistic influences on his work.
ISBN 0-316-35917-3
1. Picasso, Pablo, 1881–1973 — Juvenile
literature.   [1. Picasso, Pablo, 1881–1973.
2. Artists.   3. Painting, French.   4. Painting,
Modern — 20th century — France.   5. Art
appreciation.]   I. Title.
N6853.P5H39 1993
709'.2 — dc20
[B]   92-29653

10 9 8 7 6 5 4 3 2 1

Published simultaneously in Canada
by Little Brown & Company (Canada) Limited

Printed in Singapore

Title page photograph: Robert Doisneau, *Picasso,* 1952
Contents page art: Pablo Picasso, *Head of a Woman,* 1932, bronze statue

All works by Picasso © DACS 1992

Photographic credits

Archives Picasso / RMN: 13 right. The Art Institute of Chicago, Gift of Mrs. Gilbert W. Chapman, photograph © 1992, The Art Institute of Chicago, all rights reserved: 15 left. The Bridgeman Art Library: 19. René Burri / Magnum: 25 top. Robert Capa / Magnum: 16 top. Robert Doisneau / Rapho: title page, back cover. Collection Holger Graffman, Castellon / Scala: 24. Stephen Hahn Collection, New York: 18. Gjon Mili, *Life* Magazine © Time Warner Inc. / Katz: 29. Musée National d'Art Moderne, Centre Georges Pompidou, Paris: 16 bottom. Musée d'Orsay, Paris / RMN: 8/9. Musée Picasso, Paris / RMN: contents page, 4/5, 6 left, 7 bottom left, 20, 21, 25 bottom, 28. Musée Toulouse-Lautrec, Albi: 7 bottom. Museo de Bellas Artes, Seville: 26 right. Museo del Prado, Madrid, derechos reservados: 22/23, 27 top. Museo Picasso, Barcelona: 6 right, 27 bottom. Museum of Modern Art, New York: 12/13, 15 right. National Gallery, London, anonymous loan: front cover, 5 right. National Gallery of Art, Washington, D.C., Chester Dale Collection: 10/11. Roger-Viollet: 7 top, 14. Rosengart Collection, Lucerne: 26 left. David Seymour / Magnum: 23 right. Statens Museum for Kunst, Copenhagen: 17. Vincent van Gogh Foundation, Vincent van Gogh Museum, Amsterdam: 8 left.

Contents

Who was Picasso?

Pablo Picasso is thought of as one of the greatest artists of modern times. We probably think of Picasso and his art in this way because he has come to represent the fast and radical changes that have taken place in recent history. He lived through most of this century — with its terrible events and amazing inventions. Picasso survived two world wars and saw radios and televisions

These paintings show Picasso's amazing range of styles. The painting *Girl Holding a Dove* (*bottom right*) was made in 1901. *Women Running on the Beach* (*below*) was made twenty-one years later, in 1922.

arrive in people's lives. These wars and machines affected the way people lived, the way they worked, and the way they painted.

Picasso did not usually paint history as it happened, yet his work has become a part of history. This is because he always experimented. He drew in different ways and used unusual combinations of colors. Through Picasso's work we can understand him and see the world in his way. Picasso had an enormous amount of energy; he was not only a painter but a sculptor, set and costume designer, potter, and printmaker as well.

Early Life

Picasso was born in Málaga, on the coast of Spain, in 1881. José Ruiz Blasco, Picasso's father, was the curator of a museum and also an artist who taught drawing. As a child, Picasso learned to paint and draw with his father.

When he was fourteen, Picasso and his family moved to Barcelona, where he went to art school. As he grew older, Picasso gradually took part in the social life of the town, which often focused on the cafés, where people met.

When Picasso was nineteen, he began to visit Paris, the artistic center of Europe. By this time, he had started to paint to earn his living. Although he was a foreigner, he was among friends, for many Spanish people were living in Paris at the time. He was once again at ease in the cafés, where he could look at the life of the city around him. He painted the same kind of world that was

Torso, 1894–95.
This drawing (*above*) is Picasso's copy of a piece of classical Greek sculpture. Picasso was taught to paint and draw traditionally at an early age.

In 1896, when Picasso was fourteen, he drew this picture of his mother with pastels and crayons (*right*).

6

depicted by Henri de Toulouse-Lautrec (1864–1901), an artist he admired. Lautrec's art showed dancing girls, people laughing and joking in cafés, and life in dimly lit Parisian bars.

After his visits to Paris, Picasso returned to Barcelona, his mind filled with ideas.

The streets of Paris, like those of Barcelona, were lined with cafés where people liked to drink and talk.

Henri de Toulouse-Lautrec, *Aristide Bruant dans Son Cabaret*, 1893. Toulouse-Lautrec's posters for the theater were admired by Picasso, who knew the world they showed.

Picasso was twenty-three when this photo was taken near his studio in the Paris neighborhood of Montmartre.

After the Impressionists

By the end of the nineteenth century, many new inventions had come into the world, such as the telephone, the automobile, electricity, and photography. Art also changed because of the new ideas of a few artists. In the 1870s, the French group known as the Impressionists began to paint subjects that people had not previously thought of as being artistic. Instead of depicting legends, battles, and biblical scenes, they painted the everyday lives of ordinary people. They also painted in a looser, more vivid style than earlier artists, trying to capture in paint the way our eyes see light and color. Artists no longer had to record the world with perfect accuracy since the camera could now do that job.

In reaction to the Impressionists, the artists who came after them, called Post-Impressionists, continued to experiment in their own ways.

Monet's 1897 painting of a railway station in Paris, *Gare Saint-Lazare,* is blurred by patches of paint that look like steam.

Gauguin painted this self-portrait in 1888. He gave the portrait to his friend Vincent van Gogh as a present.

Picasso admired these artists, especially Paul Cézanne (1839–1906), Vincent van Gogh (1853–90), Paul Gauguin (1848–1903), and Toulouse-Lautrec. He tried to understand their work by adapting it into his own style. At the beginning of the twentieth century, artists felt they could be more daring. They wanted to find new subjects to paint in new ways. Picasso arrived into this exciting Parisian atmosphere, and it inspired him.

Blue and Rose

Many artists experiment with color in their painting. In the early 1900s, Picasso worked with color in a special way.

A painting, drawing, or photograph in which only one color is used is called monochrome. An artist can show how an object is shaped by making that one color darker or lighter. During this time, Picasso used a single color or just a few colors to create a mood in his paintings. These paintings comprise his Blue Period and his Rose Period as these were the main colors he used.

In his Blue Period, Picasso painted poor people and their harsh lives. The pictures look bare, and the people in them are thoughtful and still.

From 1901 to 1903, Picasso split his time between Paris and Barcelona. In 1904, he decided to settle in Paris. Even though he would spend most of his life in France, he continued to paint Spanish subjects such as folksingers and bullfights. At about this time, he also became interested in the Parisian circus and soon knew the acrobats and their families. But instead of painting the colorful world of the circus ring, he painted simple, quiet scenes of small family groups in their time away from work. The main color changed from blue to rose, so these paintings make up his Rose Period.

The paintings from the Blue and Rose periods tell about the things Picasso chose to paint. He painted real life and real people, but the way he painted often changed.

Family of Saltimbanques, 1905.
These acrobats do not speak or look at each other even though they are a family. This large oil painting was the triumph of Picasso's Blue and Rose periods.

Les Demoiselles d'Avignon
(The Women of Avignon)

In 1906, the great French artist Paul Cézanne died, and his work was exhibited in Paris. Cézanne's paintings of bathers impressed many artists, including Picasso, who began to paint his own groups of bathers.

At this time, Picasso tried to paint a portrait of his friend Gertrude Stein, but he ran into problems. He began it again and again and was never quite happy with it. Picasso had become interested in primitive sculptures and masks he had seen in exhibitions in Paris. Eventually he decided to make his friend's face look like a mask.

In 1907, Picasso painted *Les Demoiselles d'Avignon.* This picture caused great alarm. The painting shocked everyone who looked at it because the women were so ugly. The painting is difficult to understand; we cannot tell if the women are inside or outside. Are they on a stage or in a studio? Why do some of the women have mask-like faces? Is the woman in the bottom right-hand corner of the painting a copy of one of Cézanne's bathers? Originally Picasso had planned to include a sailor visiting the women, but he didn't want to add a confusing story to the picture.

Picasso was not trying to copy the world exactly as he saw it. He was trying to paint in a new way that people had never thought of before. But people did not really understand or like the painting. Picasso didn't show the work to the general public for another nine years.

Les Desmoiselles d'Avignon shows Picasso's new style. It was to change the art of the future.

12

This photograph, taken of Picasso in 1908, shows him seated in front of some primitive masks. He collected them and allowed them to influence the way he painted. The faces of the two women on the right-hand side of *Les Demoiselles d'Avignon* look like these masks.

Cubism

Soon after painting *Les Demoiselles d'Avignon*, Picasso started working with his friend Georges Braque (1882–1963). The style they created together shocked many artists as well as the public. In 1908, this style was named Cubism by the artist Henri Matisse (1869–1954) and the art critic Louis Vauxcelles.

Picasso and Braque painted the subjects of their work as if they were being seen from many

Picasso in his studio in 1928 with the paintings *Three Dancers* (1925, *right*) and *Painter and Model* (1928, *left*). He worked in different variations of his Cubist style for the rest of his life.

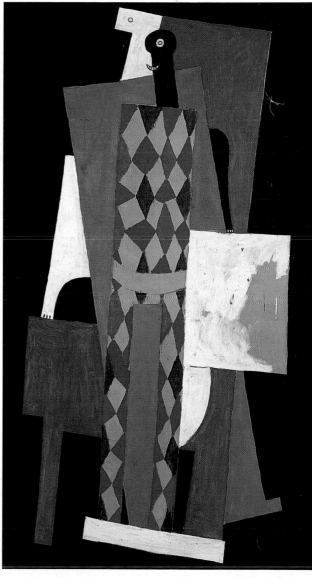

Portrait of Kahnweiler, 1910.
Picasso's friend and art dealer, Daniel-Henry Kahnweiler, posed for this portrait. His face, body, and hands, like the glass on the table next to him, are all broken up into painted fragments.

directions. This often means that the subjects are difficult to recognize. The artists painted many still lifes, paintings of objects rather than people. When they did create portraits, they were not interested in making the pictures look exactly like the people posing for the paintings.

As he had done in *Les Demoiselles d'Avignon,* Picasso made the people and objects in these paintings look flat. The objects are broken up into cubes and strange shapes. The few colors used are applied boldly.

Picasso and Braque added words and letters to their pictures. They started to stick more and more things to their paintings, such as newspaper, fabric, and even trash. This technique is called collage or *papier collé.*

Harlequin, 1915.
The flat areas of color against a plain dark background make this painting look as though it is made up of cut-out bits of paper.

15

Picasso and the Avant-Garde

In the early 1900s in Paris, artists were creating their own experimental styles. These artists composed the avant-garde. *Avant-garde* means the advance troops in a war, but in art it refers to artists who lead the way with their new ideas. Picasso became the leader of the avant-garde.

A lot of this new art shocked the public. People found it difficult to forget the art of the past. They argued about art in the newspapers and talked about it in the cafés. Picasso and other members of the avant-garde — such as Henri Matisse, Juan Gris (1887–1927), and Georges Braque — were used to these discussions.

Paris was the artistic center of Europe, and many exhibitions of new work were held there. Art dealers from all over the world bought and sold more art by avant-garde artists as interest in it grew. More galleries were created to sell this work, making the handling of art big business.

Picasso and his friends relaxing in his studio in Paris in 1944.

Luxe II, 1907–08 (*opposite*).
Henri Matisse did more than one version of this painting. He liked to reduce everything to simple, outlined shapes of color.

Juan Gris, *View onto the Bay,* 1921.
Juan Gris came to Paris in 1906. There he met Picasso and Braque and became a Cubist painter.

Painting Women

During the First World War (1914–18), Picasso
had the chance to work in the theater. He
designed the scenery and costumes for the ballet
Parade, directed by the Russian Sergei Diaghilev.
When the war was over, he returned to the
subject that inspired him all his life — women.
Picasso had many women friends and was

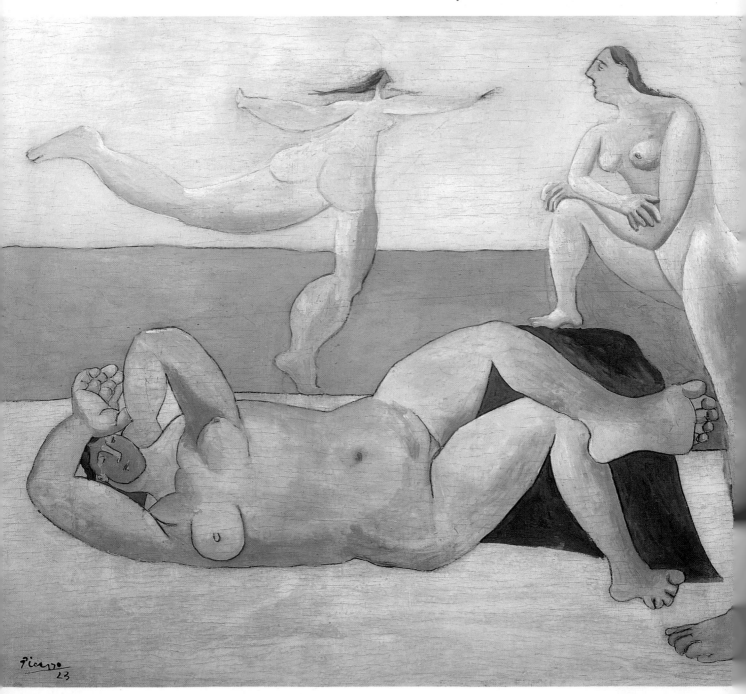

married twice. All of these women were an important part of his art.

In the 1920s, Picasso painted women differently from the way they were usually seen in art. Two and a half thousand years ago, the ancient Greeks started making what we now call classical statues, which depict perfectly beautiful men and women. This idealized approach to portraying the human form has been copied ever since. Picasso painted his own kind of classical women. But these women are big and heavy-footed, not slim and light like the figures portrayed by the Greeks. Yet the women in these paintings are still beautiful. Picasso's feelings for women ranged from love to hate, and we can see this in his paintings. Having experimented with masks earlier in his work, it was not difficult for him to change the faces in his paintings. He sometimes painted incredibly disfigured women whose features are in the wrong order or missing altogether. These paintings are so shocking that they make many viewers stop and take a second look.

Three Bathers, 1920.
The beautiful shapes of Picasso's naked women are not perfect like Greek statues (*right*). The figures in the painting look heavy, and yet the woman in the background seems to be jumping as lightly as a ballet dancer.

This Greek sculpture is called the *Venus de Milo.* It was discovered in 1820 on the Greek island of Melos. The statue is in the classical style of sculpture but dates from a later period than this.

19

Picasso the Sculptor

Sometimes Picasso concentrated on making sculpture. He said that he thought about one piece of work in many ways until he realized that it had to be sculpted rather than painted. He did not think sculpture was completely separate from painting.

Picasso's first sculptures are similar to his paintings. When Braque and Picasso created Cubism (see pages 14–15), they used collage. The first sculptures are like huge collages with real objects attached to them. He called many of these sculptures constructions because they are made of many objects (usually metal) welded together.

Materials — the things used to make paintings or sculptures — were always very important to Picasso in both types of work. He used bits of trash and everyday objects as well as clay and bronze to make sculptures. *Bull's Head* is made out of the seat and handlebars of a bicycle.

The Goat is made from many junk objects. The stomach is a wicker basket, and the legs are scrap iron. Picasso made lots of sculptures of other animals, such as owls and baboons.

Kneeling Woman, 1950 (*left*).
This small ceramic woman is boldly painted. For this type of sculpture, Picasso usually made a small bottle. Before the pottery had hardened, he bent it out of shape with his hands.

Bull's Head, 1943 (*top right*).
You can recognize the materials Picasso used in this sculpture and see them as an animal's head as well.

The Goat, 1950 (*right*).
Picasso admired interesting shapes. This goat was made out of odd objects and later covered in bronze.

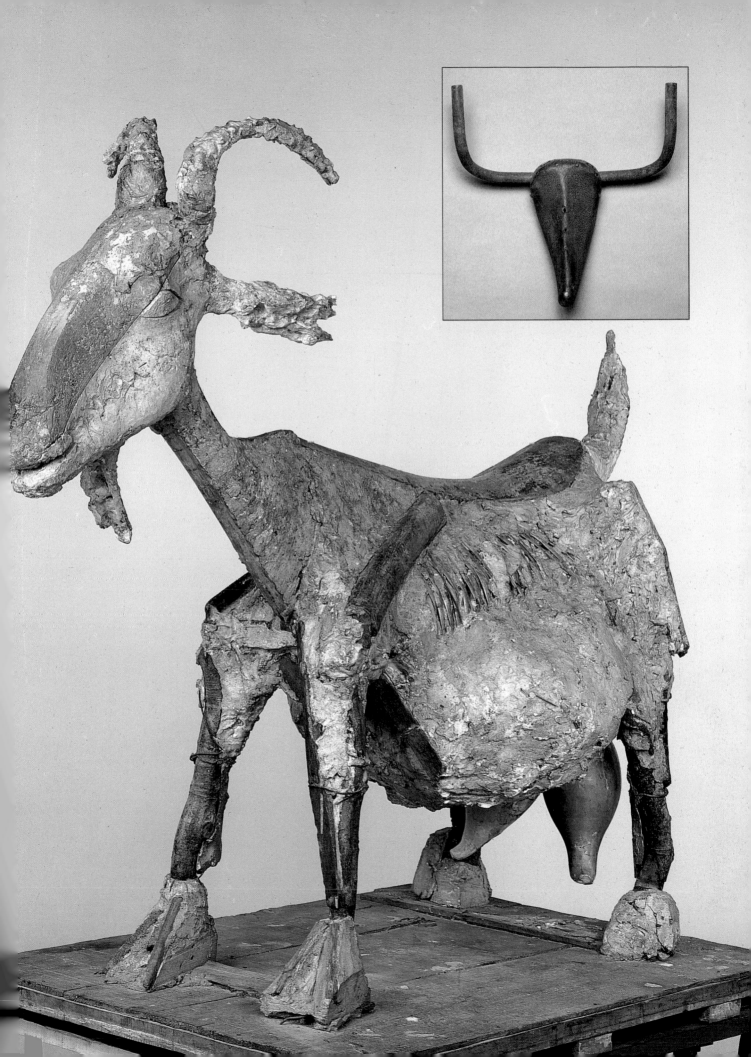

War

During the first half of this century, two great wars were fought in Europe: World War I (1914–18) and World War II (1939–45). From 1936 to 1939, Spain, Picasso's own country, was torn apart by a civil war. In a civil war, groups of people from within the same country fight each other. Picasso was very moved by the horror and suffering of these wars.

Guernica describes war in horrifying images of fear that seem to move across the length of the painting. A woman leans out of her window holding a lamp to try to see what is happening. She sees people being trampled underfoot. Another woman holds her dead baby, a horse seems to cry with despair, and a bull looks over the scene, ready to strike.

In Paris in 1937, there was to be an international exhibition of art called the *Exposition Internationale,* or World's Fair. Picasso was asked to provide a painting to represent Spain. At first he found it hard to think of a subject. Then, in 1937, the Spanish town of Guernica was bombed by General Franco in the

22

Spanish Civil War. Two thousand people were killed and the town ruined. Picasso decided to create a painting about this event for the fair. This painting is different from the rest of his work because it is about an event outside his life. Picasso usually chose more personal subjects.

Although it was inspired by a real event, Picasso's painting *Guernica* is more like a

protest against all wars in all countries and against the ability people have to make others suffer. He made many sketches and drawings for the huge painting. Picasso took out parts of the painting that would make the town recognizable so that the scene would mean something to all people who are caught up in wars.

Robert Capa, *Picasso and Guernica,* 1937.
This picture of Picasso in front of *Guernica* was taken by the photographer Robert Capa, who is famous for taking photos of real-life scenes of war. You can get some idea of how huge *Guernica* is from the picture (11 ft. 6 in. x 25 ft. 8 in.).

The
Artist
and Model

Picasso named many of his works *The Artist and His Model*. Although he painted various subjects — children, his friends, and still lifes — much of his art is of the women he loved. Here were models close at hand always ready to be painted and drawn.

Picasso was interested in the idea of the artist and model as the main subject of the painting. The artist is, after all, as important as the model. But the artist is usually not seen in the finished painting, rather like the person who takes a photograph. In painting the artist and model, Picasso showed how important he thought this relationship to be.

Artist and Model, 1957.
In this picture, Picasso has painted both himself and his model, who is posing for him in the countryside.

Sometimes Picasso painted the woman as if she was another object like a vase or a guitar. Is it possible to tell what Picasso's feelings were from his paintings? In many ways he was an Expressionist — an artist whose work tells us how he or she feels. He said, "Painting is stronger than I am. It makes me do what it likes."

In the 1930s, Picasso was painting with brilliant colors in a bold way, which made his paintings of women at this time lively and bright. Picasso always painted what he saw in a style that is like his own private language.

This is a photo of Jacqueline Roque, who became Picasso's model and later his wife (see pages 28–29).

Jacqueline in the Studio, 1957. Picasso shows Jacqueline sitting in his studio with another picture near her. Both she and the easel have become the subject of one painting.

Picasso and the Painters of the Past

Artists usually know a great deal about the work of other artists. Picasso painted in an original way but he was also aware of the painters of the past. When he was only fourteen, he won a prize for his skill at drawing and painting like one of the old masters.

As he grew older, Picasso achieved worldwide fame and was considered one of the greatest painters of the twentieth century. What did he think about some of the great painters of the past? Picasso painted his own versions of some well-known paintings, but this time he experimented. Although we can still recognize the paintings from which he copied, Picasso's versions are very different from the originals. He did not need to copy the great painters of the past, but he wanted to continue to learn from them and also to poke fun at them. Picasso was not afraid to add his own sense of humor to traditional ideas about art.

El Greco (1541–1614), *Portrait of Jorge Manual,* 1600–05 (*below*).

Portrait of a Painter, 1950, (*below right*).
Picasso deliberately copied a portrait by the Spanish painter El Greco. These paintings are hundreds of years apart and yet are obviously of the same person.

26

Diego Velázquez (1599–1660), *Las Meninas,* 1656. *Las Meninas* means the maids of honor in Spanish.

Spain's great painter of the seventeenth century, Velázquez, was a great source of inspiration for Picasso. *Las Meninas* is a scene of the Spanish royal family, some of their servants, and an artist.

The Last Years

In 1946, Picasso left Paris to live in the South of France. The sunny Mediterranean coast was similar to his Spanish homeland. This area of France has often been popular with artists. Many have gone there to paint the way the sunlight makes the colors of the landscape look bright and hot. At this time Picasso was sixty-five, and he still had twenty-five years of painting ahead of him.

When Picasso was seventy-three, he met Jacqueline Roque, and seven years later, they were married. Jacqueline and Picasso lived a quiet life in the country away from Paris. Artists, poets, sculptors, writers, and photographers came from all over the world to visit Picasso. Thanks to his

The couple in *The Kiss* appear young and full of life. In fact, this is a self-portrait of Picasso and his wife Jacqueline when he was eighty-eight (1969). The painting shows the energy he still put into his painting.

This photo shows Picasso in action, drawing not with a pen or brush but with a flashlight. The camera was able to capture his speed (1949).

energy, Picasso was always able to invent new styles and paint in new ways. As he grew older, he continued to experiment. He made hundreds of paintings a year, even when he was in his seventies and eighties.

In 1973, Picasso died at the age of ninety-one and was buried on the grounds of one of his Mediterranean houses. Of his later work, he said, "A dot for the breast, a stroke for the painter, five dashes of color for the feet, some pink and green daubs — that's enough, isn't it? What more need I do? What can I add to all that? Everything is said."

Some Key Dates

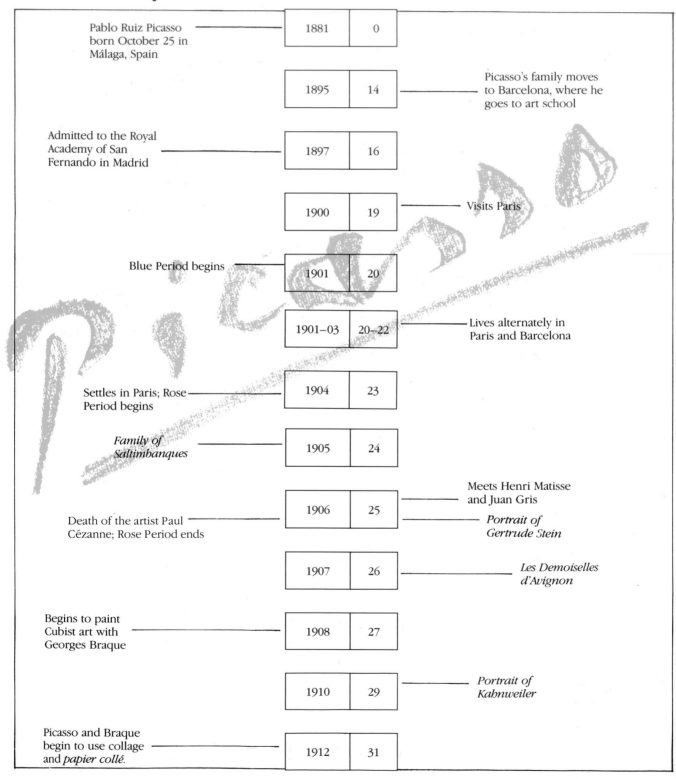

Text	Year	Age	Text
Pablo Ruiz Picasso born October 25 in Málaga, Spain	1881	0	
	1895	14	Picasso's family moves to Barcelona, where he goes to art school
Admitted to the Royal Academy of San Fernando in Madrid	1897	16	
	1900	19	Visits Paris
Blue Period begins	1901	20	
	1901–03	20–22	Lives alternately in Paris and Barcelona
Settles in Paris; Rose Period begins	1904	23	
Family of Saltimbanques	1905	24	
Death of the artist Paul Cézanne; Rose Period ends	1906	25	Meets Henri Matisse and Juan Gris / *Portrait of Gertrude Stein*
	1907	26	*Les Demoiselles d'Avignon*
Begins to paint Cubist art with Georges Braque	1908	27	
	1910	29	*Portrait of Kahnweiler*
Picasso and Braque begin to use collage and *papier collé*.	1912	31	

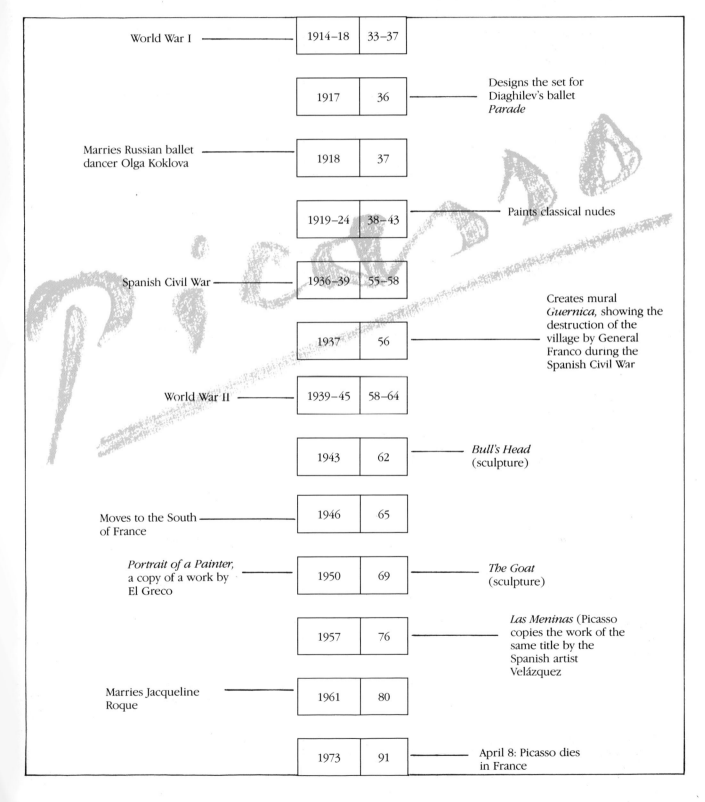

Event	Year	Age	Description
World War I	1914–18	33–37	
	1917	36	Designs the set for Diaghilev's ballet *Parade*
Marries Russian ballet dancer Olga Koklova	1918	37	
	1919–24	38–43	Paints classical nudes
Spanish Civil War	1936–39	55–58	
	1937	56	Creates mural *Guernica,* showing the destruction of the village by General Franco during the Spanish Civil War
World War II	1939–45	58–64	
	1943	62	*Bull's Head* (sculpture)
Moves to the South of France	1946	65	
Portrait of a Painter, a copy of a work by El Greco	1950	69	*The Goat* (sculpture)
	1957	76	*Las Meninas* (Picasso copies the work of the same title by the Spanish artist Velázquez)
Marries Jacqueline Roque	1961	80	
	1973	91	April 8: Picasso dies in France

Index

A **bold** number indicates that the entry is illustrated on that page. The same page often includes writing about the entry, too.

Unless otherwise stated, all of the works listed in this index are by Picasso.